JACK HANNA'S WILD BUT TRUE!

**Amazing Animal Facts
You Won't Believe!**

(But you should. Because they are true.)

Did you know that snails have four noses? Or that hippos make their own sunblock?

My name's Jack Hanna, and I didn't either until I set out to learn everything I could about animals. Today I'm the Director Emeritus of the Columbus Zoo and Aquarium and the host of two TV shows: *Jack Hanna's Into the Wild* and *Jack Hanna's Wild Countdown*. Between both jobs, I probably spend as much time with animals as I do with people—so I know firsthand how fascinating these creatures can be. I've compiled my favorite facts in this book, and they're as weird and wonderful as the critters they describe. Just see for yourself!

TABLE OF CONTENTS

SEEING IS BELIEVING .... PAGE 04

SUPER SENSES .... PAGE 24

EXTREME MEASURES .... PAGE 44

ON THE MOVE .... PAGE 66

DEADLY DETAILS .... PAGE 86

EAT UP .... PAGE 108

THAT'S GROSS! .... PAGE 128

WEIRD AND WACKY .... PAGE 150

Want to learn more? Check out *jackhanna.com* today!

SEEING IS BELIEVING

Your eyes aren't deceiving you: These are truly some of the strangest-looking creatures on the planet!

The **MEXICAN AXOLOTL** looks like larva its whole life! Unlike lizards, it doesn't lose its tadpole-like dorsal fin. Plus, its ability to regenerate body parts makes it one of the most studied salamanders in the world!

Hairy Situations

Z Z Z z z z z

SEA OTTERS have the most hair of any animal— one million hairs per square inch.

All that fur helps keep them toasty if they live in cooler water, but there's another reason for having such a thick coat: It helps them trap air inside and bob along on their backs, like a living floatie!

OTTERS hold hands when they sleep so they don't drift apart.

A **POLAR BEAR** looks white, but its hair is actually colorless. The spaces between the thick, hollow hairs bounce light, making them look white so they blend perfectly in their snowy and icy surroundings.

NAKED MOLE RATS aren't totally hairless. They have about 100 hairs on their body that are like whiskers and help them sense their surroundings.

Much like insects, naked mole rats live in large colonies with each rodent filling a role. Using their pointy teeth as well as their snouts, the worker rodents have the important job of digging the burrows for the colony to live in. When they're done digging, the worker naked mole rats also gather food for the whole colony.

EMPEROR TAMARINS
aren't born with their trademark white moustaches—

but the whiskers grow in when the monkeys are just a couple weeks old!

Even female tamarins sport the iconic stubble for which the monkeys were named, allegedly because of their facial hair's resemblance to an old German emperor's.

KAISER WILHELM

Don't worry if you see two **ZEBRAS** biting at each other! They often do so to remove one another's loose hair with their teeth. To zebras, it feels like having an itch scratched!

PORCUPINES
have soft hair beneath their sharp quills.

Under the Sea

Anglerfish look like UNDERWATER MONSTERS!

Female ANGLERFISH have glowing flesh dangling above their mouths. These personal flashlights lure dinner directly toward the fish's jaws. Now, that's what you call easy eats!

What looks like a rug but lives in the ocean? **CARPET SHARKS**, of course! Also called Wobbegongs, carpet sharks spend most of their time resting their flat, tasseled bodies on the ocean floor waiting for food to float by.

The **LEAFY SEA DRAGON** may look like seaweed, but believe it or not, it's a fish! Its looks help it hide from predators by blending in with underwater foliage.

The **MIMIC OCTOPUS** can take the shape of up to 15 different predators. It uses this skill as a defense mechanism.

UNICORNS aren't real,
but NARWHALS are!

These arctic whales
are especially unique
because they sport a tusk
for reasons no one
can figure out.
One thing scientists
do know, however,
is that <u>only</u>
MALE NARWHALS
have them.

These huge worm-like animals, called **SEA CUCUMBERS**, are related to starfish and sea urchins.

Their COOLEST TRICK is their ability to eject their internal organs for protection. They regenerate them again later!

Even though they're named after a particular food, Sea cucumbers aren't very picky eaters. Their diet is omnivorous, which means they eat a little of everything. Tiny sea animals, algae and waste materials are all fair game for these guys to feed on. Sea cucumbers gather their food using tube feet around their mouths, which look and act like tentacles.

Holiday decorations stay up year-round in

Unlike the evergreens for which these critters were named, **CHRISTMAS TREE WORMS** come in all kinds of colors, such as orange, yellow, blue and white.

the tropical waters these animals call home.

The tentacles that grow from their bodies help the worms breathe and eat.

Even though you can't see them, harmless microscopic shrimp called COPEPODS live in some drinking water.

Handy Noses

The bigger a male **PROBOSCIS MONKEY'S** nose, the better!

It helps them sound **LOUD** warning calls when their group is in danger.

Plus, a big schnoz gets a lot of attention from female monkeys.

The *Jack Hanna's Into the Wild* film crew filmed these fascinating Proboscis monkeys while in Malaysia in 2009!

AFRICAN ELEPHANT

Although it looks a lot different than most animals', an **ELEPHANT**'s trunk is actually a long nose used for smelling, breathing, trumpeting, drinking and, with the help of finger-like features on the end, grabbing. Plus, the trunk alone is controlled by 10,000 different muscles!

I saw this magnificent African elephant while in Botswana filming for *Jack Hanna's Into the Wild* at Chobe National Park in 2011. Did you know African elephants, which are a little larger than their Asian elephant cousins, are the largest land animals on Earth? But the elephants differ in size only a little bit, so you can tell them apart by their ears. An African elephant's ears are shaped like the continent of Africa, while Asian elephants have smaller, more rounded ears.

SpotsandStripes

Don't let the stripes fool you, the **OKAPI** is related to the giraffe, not the zebra. It's the animal's only living kin, though the cousins live in different habitats.

Some people think the **GIRAFFE**'s pattern is camouflage. Whether or not that's the pattern's purpose, it works that way! Many people have reported mistaking giraffes for old dead trees!

In addition to their fur, **SKUNKS'** skin is striped, too. And the patterns vary from skunk to skunk!

As a group, they look the same, but every **ZEBRA**'s stripe pattern is different!

Every tiger's stripe <u>pattern</u> is different, too!

TIGERS come in a variety of colors. They can have white fur with black stripes, orange fur with black stripes, orange fur with blonde stripes or even white fur with white stripes.

BENGAL TIGER

BLACK PANTHERS are actually melanistic leopards. Being melanistic means they have lots of extra black pigment that accounts for their color.

If you look closely, you can see they still have spots just like other leopards.

Best in Show

A female **CAIRN TERRIER** named Terry played Toto in *The Wizard of Oz*, and the Taco Bell dog was portrayed by a female **CHIHUAHUA** named Gidget.

Every year in Huacho, Peru, there's a **GUINEA PIG** Festival, which includes a costume contest.

The first **WESTMINSTER KENNEL CLUB** dog show was held in 1876 to celebrate America's 100th birthday.

Sweden has a competition called Kaninhoppning. In English, that means **"RABBIT SHOW JUMPING."**

HeadsandTails

OWLS can rotate their necks up to 270 degrees in each direction. That's almost a full circle!

They can do this because their heads are connected by only one socket, and blood can flow to and from their heads via multiple paths.

BALD EAGLES aren't bald! They got their name from the Old English word "balde," which means white, the color of the feathers on their heads.

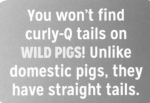

You won't find curly-Q tails on WILD PIGS! Unlike domestic pigs, they have straight tails.

PIGS roll in mud to keep cool because they can't sweat. Otherwise, they're pretty clean animals.

DOMESTIC PIG

Salamander tails never stop growing, and they can regenerate if severed by a predator.

SUPER SENSES

The way some animals take in the world is just plain wacky! See for yourself.

PLATYPUSES have a sixth sense! Their bills can detect electrical fields created when their prey moves. Sharks have a similar skill.

Spectacular Smellers

SAND TIGER SHARK

Two-thirds of a SHARK's brain is dedicated to smell, and it can smell a single drop of blood in the water from a mile away.

Because they live in the water, you might wonder why sand tiger sharks are named after something you find on land. The name comes from their preference to make habitats near shorelines, where sand exists. Plus, unlike other sharks, sand tiger sharks actually come up to gulp air!

RATS' great sense of smell works in stereo, too. In fact, they're so talented that researchers in Cambodia are training them to sniff out land mines and other explosives.

COWS have a surprisingly keen sense of smell.

They can smell stuff from **5 OR 6 MILES AWAY.**

POLAR BEARS can smell a seal under ice from half a mile away. Even better, they can smell a seal under snow from a full mile away.

Most marine birds use their eyesight to spot supper, but the **ALBATROSS** can smell them. It catches a whiff of its prey while flying over the ocean, then makes a deep dive for dinner.

A **SALMON**'s sense of smell is thousands of times better than a dog's.

A **HORSE** isn't laughing when his mouth is opened and his upper lip is curled...

He's *sniffing*, using a technique called **FLEHMEN**, which enhances his sense of **SMELL**.

Snails have 4 noses.

1 2 4 3 4

SNAKES and lizards use their tongues to smell! Each fork is like a nose that senses chemicals in the air. If a snake or lizard identifies a certain chemical balance in one fork, it knows to follow that fork to its prey.

MOJAVE RATTLESNAKE

The scent BINTURONGS use to mark their territory smells like buttered popcorn!

POP CORN

POP CORN

Eye Spy

CHAMELEONS see double—literally! By rotating and focusing both eyes on two things at the same time, the lizard can see multiple objects at once!

JUMPING SPIDERS can see colors we can't! Jumping spiders don't stop at the red, green and other colors humans see. They can also see ultraviolet, or energy that is like light but invisible to the human eye.

MOSQUITOES have infrared vision. That means they can see heat!

BUTTERFLIES have 12,000 eyes!

FOUR-EYED FISH only have two eyes. They got their name because their eyes are partitioned so they can see underwater and above water at the same time.

HORSES can see nearly 360 degrees at once because their eyes are on the sides of their heads.

REINDEER
can see
ultraviolet light.

To them, black lights, which emit UV light, would appear bright like a lamp.

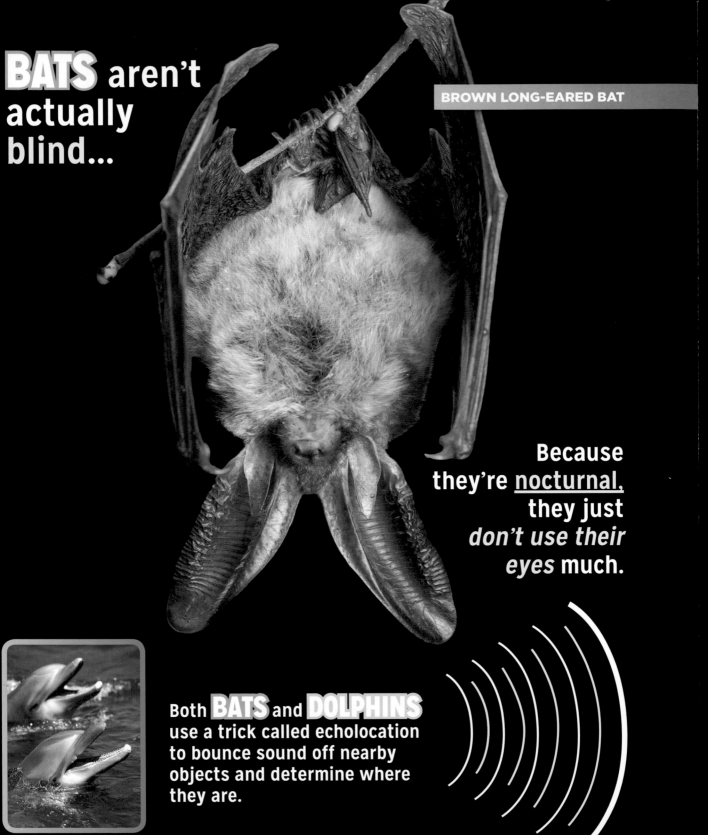

BATS aren't actually blind...

BROWN LONG-EARED BAT

Because they're <u>nocturnal,</u> they just *don't use their eyes* much.

Both **BATS** and **DOLPHINS** use a trick called echolocation to bounce sound off nearby objects and determine where they are.

AFRICAN ELEPHANT

ELEPHANTS' eyes aren't great. Instead of sight, they primarily depend on their trunks to orient themselves.

Because the Slovenian and Croatian caves where it lives are so dark, the OLM SALAMANDER never evolved eyes.

Even though olm salamanders don't have eyes, the skin where their eyes would be is still sensitive to light. Luckily, they don't have to worry about light too often. When it comes to hunting prey, the olm salamander's other senses like their hearing and smell work extra hard. Amazingly, they can live up to 10 years without food if they need to!

The **PANDA** is one of the only animals that is not a primate but has opposable thumbs. Over time, pandas have evolved a bony outgrowth on their wrists used to grip bamboo.

Pandas certainly put their opposable thumbs to good use living in the mountainous regions of China. These areas are filled with high bamboo forests, and in the summer pandas will sometimes climb up slopes as high as 13,000 feet to feed! But climbing trees is not all these mammals are good at. When in water, pandas are pretty good swimmers, too!

ORANGUTANS
are
ticklish.

Elephants have nothing on **STAR NOSED MOLES!** They have 22 tiny trunks, which gives their noses a sense of touch about six times better than a human hand. The supersensitive organs allow them to identify prey in less than half a second!

ALLIGATOR skin is super sensitive and can detect even minute vibrations.

SEALS' whiskers can detect fish swimming up to 600 feet away.

All Ears

The **PRAYING MANTIS** is the only known animal with just one ear! It's hidden deep within the insect's chest.

TAWNY OWLS can determine the speed and direction of a mouse scurrying across the forest floor in a tenth of a second.

The **GREATER WAX MOTH** boasts the best hearing in the animal kingdom. They can pick up frequencies more than 15 times higher than those humans can hear.

A **CAT**'s ear works like a sophisticated satellite dish:

It rotates up to 180 degrees to pick up even the quietest sounds.

180°

Even though dogs are known for picking up high-pitched whistles that are silent to humans, cats are comparatively <u>much better</u> at it.

Elephants can hear storms up to

An **ELEPHANT**'s trunk and feet help them hear. They're packed with receptors that pick up vibrations that make low-frequency sounds.

150 miles away.

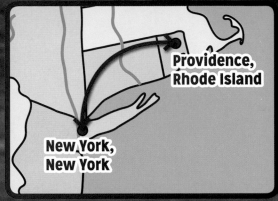

That's about the distance from New York City to Providence, Rhode Island!

Asian elephants at my home, the Columbus Zoo and Aquarium, always enjoy a quick dip on a hot day!

Not only are an elephant's ears great for helping them hear distant sounds, they also keep them cool in hot climates. Elephants flap their ears like big fans to cool down the blood in their many blood vessels. Once the temperature of their blood goes down, their bodies will feel much colder. Or, they can always just take a quick dip in the water!

Different Tastes

OCTOPUSES have taste buds on each of their 1,800 suction cups!

FLIES taste with their feet. If they like what they land on, they'll take a bite with their mouths.

BUTTERFLIES taste with their feet, too, but for a different reason. They use the skill to detect poisonous plants and avoid death by dinner.

CATS don't have a sweet tooth. Members of the cat family can't taste sweet things.

WHITE-CROWNED SPARROWS can tell which foods are most nutritious and eat accordingly.

HERBIVORES have more taste buds than CARNIVORES. This helps the veggie eaters determine whether specific plants are dangerous because they can taste toxins.

BIRDS have fewer taste buds than MAMMALS.

For example, CHICKENS have about 30, while COWS have about 25,000!

With a maximum shell length of about 4 inches, the **SPECKLED PADLOPER** is the smallest known tortoise in the world.

EXTREME MEASURES

From huge to tiny, you won't believe how these awesome animals size up!

Being small is an advantage for the speckled padloper. Because they live in dry, arid habitats, these tiny tortoises need reliable shelter to shield themselves from the hot summer sun. The speckled padloper's shell size allows it to easily slip into rock crevices to cool down in the shade when temperatures rise to 100 degrees or above.

Calling All Whales

A newborn **BLUE WHALE** can be longer than an adult elephant.

BLUE WHALES have the largest heart of <u>any</u> animal.

It would take about 3,000 female human hearts to equal the weight of one blue whale's!

The average female human heart weighs about ½ a pound, while a whale's weighs roughly 1,500 pounds.

Blue whales are the biggest animal on Earth!

SPERM WHALES have the world's heftiest brains!

The heaviest **SPERM WHALE** brain ever recorded was **17.2 pounds.** That's nearly _8 times heavier_ than the average human brain!

World's Tallest

GIRAFFES are the tallest animal in the world.

Even their **babies** are **taller** than most adult humans!

A **giraffe's** tongue is about **21 inches long**, nearly the length of 2 foot-long sandwiches stacked end-to-end!

It would take roughly **18 GIRAFFES** stacked on top of one another to match the height of the Statue of Liberty.

The largest **GIANT SQUID** ever discovered was **59 FEET LONG**—about ½ the length of a football field. Plus, its eyes were as big as beach balls! The giant squid has the largest eyes of any creature in the animal kingdom.

Speaking of big eyes, **HORSES** have the largest of any mammal on land!

OSTRICHES are the heaviest and tallest birds in the world. Males can weigh up to 350 pounds and stand up to 9 feet tall!

OSTRICHES have the largest eyes of any bird. One of their eyes is about <u>twice as wide across as a quarter.</u> Their eyes are even bigger than horses'!

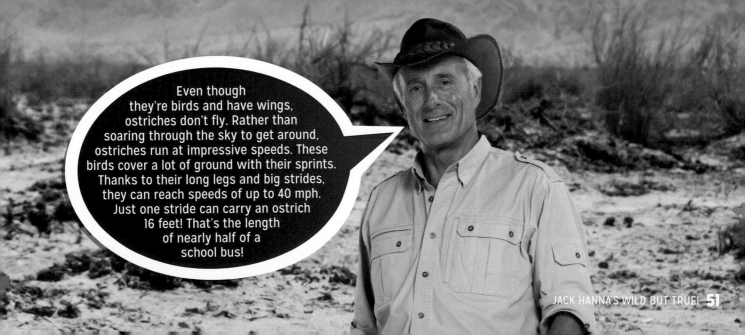

Even though they're birds and have wings, ostriches don't fly. Rather than soaring through the sky to get around, ostriches run at impressive speeds. These birds cover a lot of ground with their sprints. Thanks to their long legs and big strides, they can reach speeds of up to 40 mph. Just one stride can carry an ostrich 16 feet! That's the length of nearly half of a school bus!

Super Small

Each drop of rain weighs about 50 times more than a MOSQUITO.

At birth, a GIANT PANDA is smaller than an adult mouse.

Adult pandas grow to more than 200 POUNDS!

Baby kangaroos are called *joeys.*

At 1 month old, a baby **KANGAROO** is barely bigger than a jelly bean.

A baby **POSSUM** can be as small as a honeybee!

Joeys stay in their mothers' pouches for almost a year!

CHIHUAHUAS are
the smallest dogs
in the world.

Even the biggest members
of the breed weigh fewer
than SEVEN POUNDS.

FLEAS have wings, but they <u>can't fly.</u> Instead, they **JUMP!**

FLEAS can jump up to 200 times their height. That would be like a **6-foot-tall** man jumping to the roof of the **EMPIRE STATE BUILDING.**

SLOTHS clock about <u>20 hours</u> of sleep each day.

RING RING RING RING RING RING

Even when they are awake, **SLOTHS** move only short distances, and they do so very slowly. In fact, they're so sluggish, algae grows on their fur!

We were lucky to snap this shot while filming for *Jack Hanna's Into the Wild* in Panama in 2013—the baby was wide awake!

Newborn DOLPHINS sleep just a few seconds at a time. When dolphins sleep, they use only about half of their brains because, for them, breathing isn't an involuntary reflex. If they fell entirely asleep, they'd forget to breathe!

Breathing is something dolphins have to think about no matter what they're doing. Even when they're swimming, these intelligent mammals take breaks to get air above water about two or three times a minute. Dolphins usually swim at speeds around 19 miles per hour. You'd want to catch your breath too after swimming that fast!

Parts and Pieces

Some SEA STARS have as many as 40 arms. In fact, one kind even has 50!

Full-grown SEA STARS can be smaller than a dime, bigger than a garbage can lid and every size in between!

CROWN-OF-THORNS STARFISH

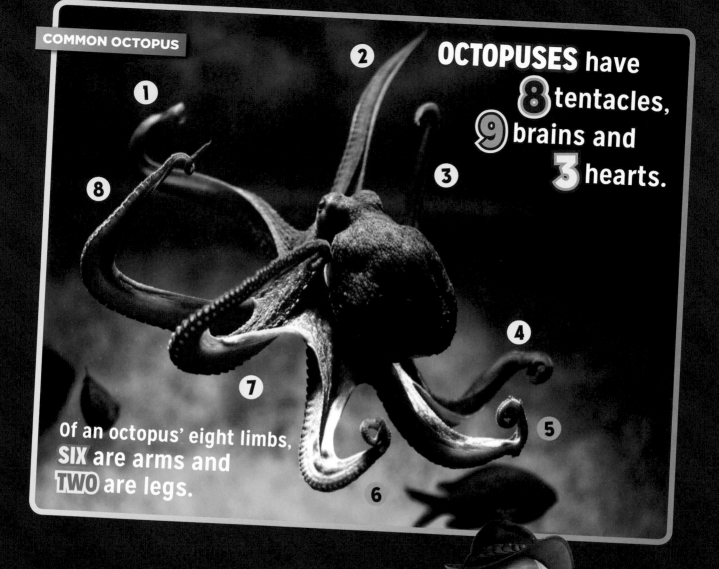

COMMON OCTOPUS

OCTOPUSES have **8** tentacles, **9** brains and **3** hearts.

Of an octopus' eight limbs, **SIX** are arms and **TWO** are legs.

The mimic octopus is one sea creature that puts its multiple limbs and brains to particularly good use. To take the shape of a lion fish, for example, the octopus swims with its arms spread out wide and trailing behind to imitate the fish's poisonous fins.

A **WALRUS** can have as many as **700** whiskers.

Although walrus whiskers can grow up to a <u>foot long</u>, rubbing against the sea floor usually reduces the <u>whiskers to nubs</u>.

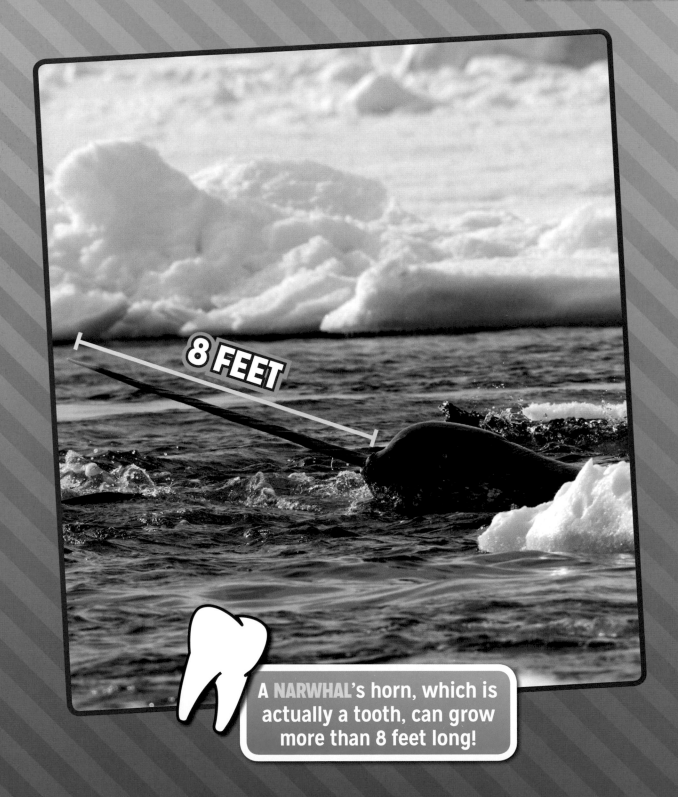

8 FEET

A **NARWHAL**'s horn, which is actually a tooth, can grow more than 8 feet long!

The OCEAN SUNFISH lays more eggs per season than any other animal: 300 million!

At nearly 1 pound, a **BROWN KIWI** egg weighs about as much as six large chicken eggs. The bird itself is only about the size of a chicken.

Ocean sunfish are better at growing than any animal in the ocean. At birth, these fish are smaller than the center of a Cheerio, but fully grown they can weigh up to 5,000 pounds! Scientists believe ocean sunfish grow this large by eating a steady diet of jellyfish. Despite being gigantic, ocean sunfish are preyed on by sea lions, who rip off their fins for food.

Mouthing Off

The GIANT ANTEATER has the <u>longest</u> tongue in relation to its body size of <u>any mammal</u>.

ANTEATERS
don't have any teeth.

BEAVERS' front teeth never stop growing.

LEMON SHARK

SHARKS never stop growing new teeth, and some species have as many as eight rows.

GIRAFFES have the same number of teeth as humans: 32.

"BRACHIATE" is a word that describes the way primates swing from branch to branch with their arms.

ON THE MOVE

Whether they're creeping, crawling, swimming or flying, these wild things are on their way!

Male orangutans usually prefer to travel alone, unlike other apes, such as chimpanzees. When brachiating through the forest, male orangutans howl loudly. This is sometimes known as a "long call," and orangutans use it to warn others to stay out of their way as they swing between branches. These calls are so loud, they can be heard 1.2 miles away!

World's Fastest

The **PEREGRINE FALCON** is the FASTEST ANIMAL ON EARTH. It can reach **117 MILES PER HOUR** while diving.

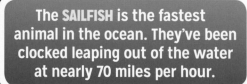

The **SAILFISH** is the fastest animal in the ocean. They've been clocked leaping out of the water at nearly 70 miles per hour.

The **CHEETAH** is the fastest land animal on the planet. They can run up to 70 miles per hour!

At the Columbus Zoo's "Heart of Africa" region, you can see them in action sprinting around the watering hole!

It's easy to think of turtles as slow, but that's not always the case. The fastest turtle is the **LEATHERBACK**. They've been clocked swimming at speeds above 20 miles per hour.

Quick Learners

As soon as
SEA TURTLES
hatch on the beach,
they follow the
light of the moon
toward the ocean,
where they'll spend
the rest of their lives.

A newborn **GIRAFFE** can walk about an hour after it's born.

Baby **SEAHORSES** float together in small groups, clinging to each other using their tails.

OTTERS get their first swim lessons from their mothers when they're about 2 months old.

Once otters become comfortable swimmers, they swim on their backs. Sometimes, though, they switch to their stomachs, kind of like human swimmers who use both techniques. The size of the groups otters travel in can range from around 10 all the way to 100. These groups are called rafts since otters spend a lot of time floating together.

Wet and Wild

FLYING FISH can soar <u>4 feet</u> out of the water and glide for distances of up to <u>655 feet</u>—nearly the length of TWO FULL FOOTBALL FIELDS.

A group of **JELLYFISH** is called a smack or a bloom.

SEAHORSES sometimes get too exhausted to swim.

FRENCH ANGELFISH

A group of fish is called a school. Fish often travel in schools to stay safe.

OLIVE RIDLEY SEA TURTLES migrate hundreds or thousands of miles each year to return to the beaches where they were born and lay eggs of their own.

Some lizards, like the **BASILISK**, can walk on water.

Unlike most cats, **JAGUARS** don't avoid water. They're good swimmers.

BALD EAGLES
can swim.

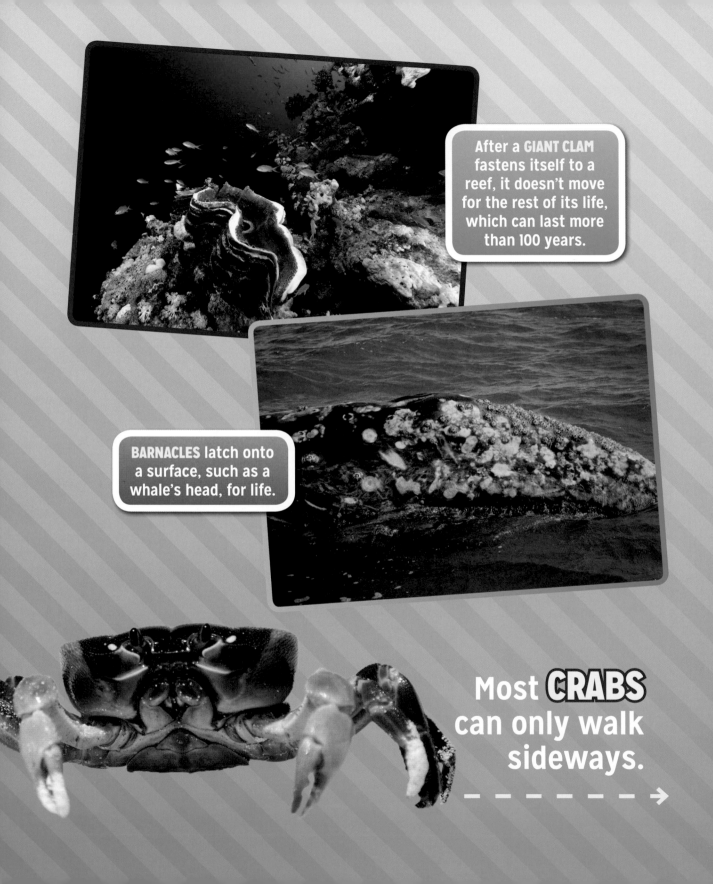

After a GIANT CLAM fastens itself to a reef, it doesn't move for the rest of its life, which can last more than 100 years.

BARNACLES latch onto a surface, such as a whale's head, for life.

Most **CRABS** can only walk sideways.

PENGUINS slide over ice on their stomachs because it's faster and easier than waddling with their short, stubby legs. Their preferred mode of transportation is **SWIMMING.**

PENGUINS can't fly. BUT THAT'S OK! Underwater, their strong, hard wings propel them through the water. They swim up to <u>3,100 miles</u> per year.

Sky High

MONARCH BUTTERFLIES migrate to Mexico each winter.

MEXICO

If **BUTTERFLIES** get too cold, they have to warm their wings in the sun before flying.

BEES need to land on about **2 MILLION FLOWERS** to make one pound of honey.

More than **TWO MILLION** U.S. animals travel *via airplane* each year.

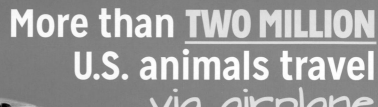

A dog named **LAIKA** was the first living creature in orbit. The Soviet Union launched her into space on November 3, 1957.

Some GEESE can fly as high as jets!

FLYING SQUIRRELS use the stretchy pieces of skin between their arms and legs to sail through treetops.

The SOOTY SHEARWATER has the longest migration of any animal. It flies from New Zealand to the North Pacific Ocean every summer, clocking nearly 40,000 miles per year.

HUMMINGBIRDS
are the only birds that can fly
backward.

Check out this hummingbird filmed for *Jack Hanna's Into the Wild* in Ecuador in 2015.

For hummingbirds, flying is the only way to get around! Hummingbirds cannot walk or hop like other birds do because their feet have evolved to be smaller, allowing them to fly faster. And it works! Hummingbirds can reach 60 mph on a dive!

Land Lovers

KANGAROOS can't walk <u>backward.</u> Their oddly shaped legs and bulky tails are to blame.

KANGAROOS can't move their hind legs separately, either.

COTTONTAIL RABBITS hop away from predators in a zigzag pattern.

HORSES can travel up to 100 miles in a day.

EARTHWORMS can burrow as deep as 6½ feet in one day.

That's deeper than the average grown-up man is tall!

MOUNTAIN GOATS
can reach nearly
12 FEET HIGH
in one jump.

My wife Sue snapped this photo while we were hiking in Glacier National Park!

The prehistoric giant **SHORT-FACED KANGAROO** was the largest hopping animal ever to exist. It weighed more than 440 pounds.

While climbing, **SNAKES** push on tree trunks with the force of more than **9** times their body weight.

EMERALD TREE BOA

KINKAJOUS can rotate their feet backward to easily run up and down tree branches and trunks.

LAND TORTOISES are super slow. Some walk at only about ½ mile per hour, compared to humans, who walk a little less than 3 miles per hour.

Filming for *Jack Hanna's Into the Wild* is always a fun experience—when we went to the Galapagos Islands in 2015, we couldn't pass up a chance to see these tortoises in person!

Most of the time, land tortoises choose to travel by themselves. But that doesn't mean they don't buddy up every now and again. When tortoises do roam in small groups, it's called a creep! And even though they move really slowly, tortoises usually know where they're going. They have a good sense of direction and can also recognize local landmarks.

DEADLY DETAILS

These facts are almost as ferocious as the creatures they describe!

Small But Mighty

A form of Kung Fu is named after the **PRAYING MANTIS** because the insect is such a quick, aggressive predator.

KOMODO DRAGONS, like this one at the Columbus Zoo and Aquarium, use their saliva, which contains potentially harmful bacteria, to weaken larger prey.

BOMBARDIER BEETLES can shoot hot poison from their rear ends 500 times per second! The little bugs can even aim the poison to make sure they hit their marks—which are usually attackers or potential threats.

At only two inches long, the golden poison dart frog is one of the most toxic animals on the planet. Just one frog has enough venom to kill 10 grown men!

Biggest Biters

Four tons of pressure are pushed through every square centimeter of tooth when a 3-meter-long GREAT WHITE SHARK bites. What's that mean? It would be like the tip of your fingers delivering the weight of four small cars when you touched someone!

Some scientists think ZEBRA's stripes might help prevent insect bites.

WOLVES can bite with a SUPER STRONG jaw pressure of 1,500 pounds per square inch.

(That's like a quarter pushing down on your hand with the weight of a cow!)

Believe It Or Not

Guinness World Records named the **HONEY BADGER** "the most fearless animal on the planet." They often drive lions away from their prey!

AMERICAN WILD PIGS

usually use their speed to escape predators, but if cornered, they become <u>vicious.</u> Their razor-sharp lower tusks, which never stop growing, can easily slice through a **3-INCH TREE ROOT.**

Even after they're dead, **JELLYFISH** can still sting.

A person is more likely to be killed by a a FALLING COCONUT than a SHARK.

Hungry Hunters

The **SIBERIAN LYNX** often hunts prey **3 to 4** times its size.

Given the chance, the cat can even bring down a 500-pound REINDEER!

AFRICAN WILD DOGS are among the best predators on their continent. On average, 80 PERCENT of their hunts result in a kill, compared to 10 PERCENT of lions' hunts.

A pack of
AFRICAN WILD DOGS
can consume a gazelle
in just 10 MINUTES!

Tricky Predators

BOA CONSTRICTORS hang from tree branches and cave openings to snatch bats as they fly by.

The HARPY EAGLE can turn its head upside down, which helps the bird get a good look at its potential dinner. From its silent tree perch, the eagle can stalk prey for up to 23 hours!

Much like the way dogs herd sheep, BOTTLENOSE DOLPHINS herd fish, and then they eat them!

FEMALE BLACK WIDOW SPIDERS

sometimes kill and eat their mates.
Other than this deadly ritual,
black widows spend
their time <u>alone.</u>

Not only are they a threat to their own kind, but female black widow spiders are also dangerous to humans. They're considered to be the most venomous spider in all of North America, containing venom that's 15 times more toxic than that of a rattlesnake. However males and young black widows are not venomous.

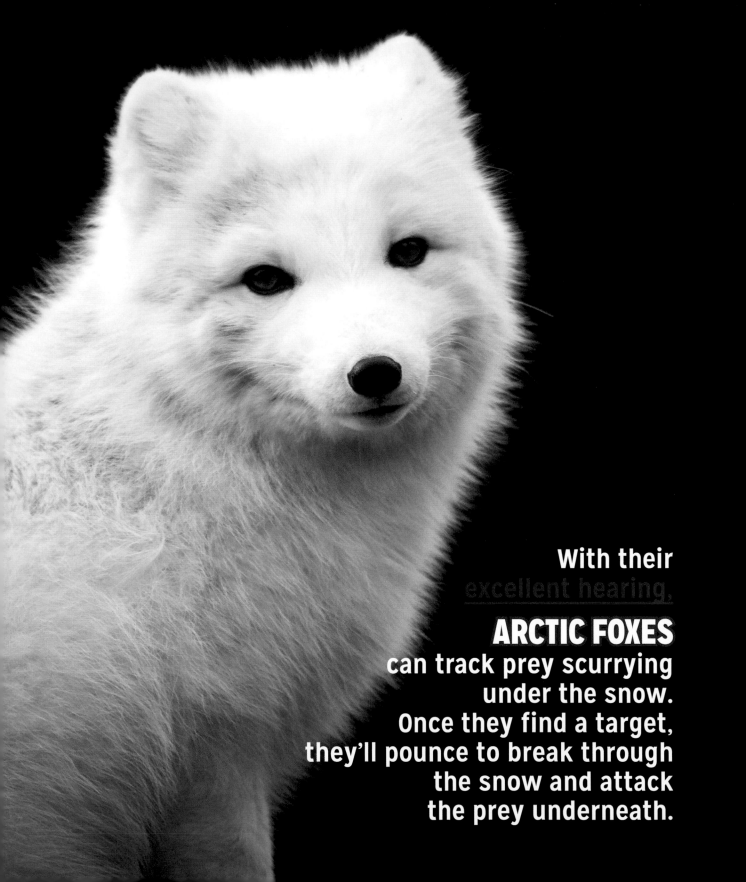

With their
excellent hearing,

ARCTIC FOXES
can track prey scurrying
under the snow.
Once they find a target,
they'll pounce to break through
the snow and attack
the prey underneath.

While sprinting, **CHEETAHS** can change direction in midair to follow their prey.

Unlike the cheetah, which chases prey, the **SERVAL** takes a huge leap into the air and lands on its victim with all its weight.

Servals live in most parts of Africa, where they have plenty of options for prey. These cats aren't too picky when it comes to eating, either. Reptiles, rodents, birds and insects are all commonly on the menu when servals hunt for food. Sometimes, they even dip their long front legs into water to catch fish for dinner!

Deadly Doses

The **ANEMONE** may look like a pretty sea plant, but it uses its venom-filled tentacles to stab prey with a neurotoxin, rendering them helpless and ready to be eaten.

Some of humanity's most deadly infectious diseases are carried by MOSQUITOES.

Venom and poison are different. Venom is injected, while poison is eaten or absorbed.

PLATYPUSES are one of the only venomous mammals. They use spurs on their back limbs to shoot venom at other males—but the spray isn't lethal to humans.

BLACK MAMBA SNAKES—which are actually gray but get their names from their black mouths—have very fast, strong venom, which contains a neurotoxin stronger than morphine.

You can tell the deadly **CORAL SNAKE** from its non-venomous look-alike, the **SCARLET KING SNAKE**, remember this rhyme:

CORAL SNAKE

SCARLET KING SNAKE

"**RED** on **YELLOW**, kill a fellow; **RED** on **BLACK**, venom lack."

Escape Artists

If nabbed by predators, the **PEACOCK'S** feathers pull out _easily,_ which allows them to fly away from danger.

KANGAROOS notify one another about approaching danger by thumping their feet on the ground.

KIWIS let out shrieks that are half-scream, half-whistle to keep track of one another and scare away predators. The bird got its name from the shriek, which sounds like...

To escape hungry leopards, **RED RIVER HOGS** swim underwater, coming up to catch their breath about every 15 seconds.

KEE-WEE, KEE-WEE!

CROCODILES first appeared on Earth about 230 million years ago. They've outlived dinosaurs and ice ages, and the only real threat to their existence is humans.

While crocodiles have been known to attack humans from time to time, this is not their nature. American crocodiles, specifically, are not nearly as aggressive as their Australian crocodile cousins. They are shy and usually unseen by humans. Instead of snacking on people, crocodiles enjoy eating small fish, birds and reptiles.

Playing Dead

BABY BROWN SNAKES freeze in the face of danger as a form of <u>protection</u>.

POSSUMS sometimes go into shock and turn limp when they're stressed, just like a person who has fainted. The reaction comes in handy in the face of predators, who think the possum is dead and pass on the potential dinner.

JEWEL WASPS lay their eggs in the bodies of cockroaches. When the eggs hatch and the larvae leave their host, the cockroach stands guard over the wasp babies.

Not all animals play dead to avoid predators—some do so to capture prey! The **CENTRAL AMERICAN CICHLID** plays dead to attract other fish to eat—ones that would otherwise attack it. The cichlid even has markings that make it look like a decaying fish. Talk about a trickster!

FLAMINGOS get their iconic color from their diets of shrimp and algae, which contain carotenoid, a substance that contributes to the birds' pink pigment.

EAT UP

These animals make mealtime awesome.

Although they're too salty for most other animals, big, shallow lakes in countries such as Mexico and Chile are home to flamingos. Algae and small crustaceans live there, too. Without competition for food, flamingos basically have an exclusive buffet right at their feet!

Big Appetites

A **GIANT PANDA**'s diet is **99 percent bamboo**. They can spend up to 16 hours each day eating as much as 40 POUNDS OF IT.

The **PYGMY SHREW** eats about 1.3 times its body weight every day.

COWS can consume 90 pounds of food per day.

Anteaters can eat a combined total of 35,000 ants and termites per day.

Ants have **2** stomachs.

1 INCH

An **ANTEATERS** mouth is only 1 INCH WIDE

A blue whale's stomach can hold 2,200 POUNDS OF KRILL.

Although they sometimes enjoy small snacks of berries and rodents, GRIZZLY BEARS often dine on massive meals of moose!

EAT UP

SHARKS are hungry even before they're born and develop teeth while inside their mothers' tummies.

ELEPHANTS can eat about 300 pounds of food in one day.

People Pleasers

BEES produce two to three times more honey than they need. More for us!

= 1 BILLION GALLONS

COWS in the United States produce a total of <u>21 billion gallons of milk</u> each year. That's nearly <u>666 gallons per second!</u>

Ground-up insects are sometimes used to color red foods. They're often listed as cochineal, carmine, carminic acid, Natural Red 4 or E120 in the ingredient list.

Raw TERMITES taste like pineapple.

Termites are known for eating wood, but how do these little bugs stomach such a splintery thing? Their bodies are built to digest cellulose, which is the organic material found in wood. Rather than dine alone, termites munch on wood in groups called colonies. These colonies are so wood-hungry, they eat 24 hours a day!

Thirst Quenchers

CAMELS
can travel up to **100 miles** in the desert without water.

A person is supposed to drink at least ¼ gallon of water each day. **CAMELS** drink **80 times** that —20 GALLONS—each time they're thirsty. Then, they don't drink again for a couple weeks.

My wife, Sue, and I love to visit *the Wilds*, a 10,000-acre conservation center in Cumberland, Ohio and a partner of the Columbus Zoo. Filled with giraffes, rhinos, zebras, camels and more—you never know what you'll find when you go on safari at *the Wilds*!

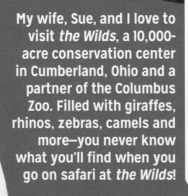

KOALAS don't need to drink water. Instead, they get their water from the eucalyptus leaves they eat.

Dinnertime Technique

FROGS' eyes help them swallow. Closing their eyes pushes food down their throats.

RED EYED TREE FROG

GREAT HORNED OWL

Because they don't have teeth, **OWLS** can't chew their food. Instead, they rip it apart or swallow it whole.

The **PLATYPUS** doesn't have teeth, either. Instead, it grinds its food between the tough pads on its upper and lower jaws.

To find food, platypuses use their snouts, which look like duck bills. These unique snouts have thousands of receptors that allow the platypus to detect prey. Once they've located lunch, they scoop up worms, shellfish and insects with their big bills and store the tasty findings in their cheek pouches.

LEAFCUTTER ANTS' jaws vibrate 1,000 times per second to chew leaves. We couldn't believe our luck when we saw these in person while filming for *Jack Hanna's Into the Wild* in Panama in 2013.

CHIPMUNKS
have pouches in their cheeks to store their food, which can include bird eggs, berries and nuts.

CAMELS chew in a figure-eight motion.

SNAKES can unhinge their jaws to swallow meals *BIGGER THAN THEIR MOUTHS.*

Scavenger Hunt

Hyenas can digest bones.

A scavenger is an animal who eats dead or decaying materials.

Racoons, Hyenas and Cockroaches are examples of scavengers.

VULTURES can eat rotten meat because they have special chemicals in their stomachs that kill the bacteria that would make other animals sick.

TASMANIAN DEVILS are sometimes called "vacuum cleaners of the forest" because they often eat animals that are already dead.

Tasmanian devils are carnivorous, meaning they eat other animals—and they are far from picky. They eat wallabies, reptiles, birds, small mammals and insects. In farming areas, tasmanian devils eat the carcasses of sheep and cattle. When groups of tasmanian devils eat carcasses, they make loud noises to show their dominance.

Food for Thought

MACAWS counter poisonous seeds by eating clay.

If they swallow something toxic, the clay helps them eliminate harmful substances from their bodies.

SLOTH BEARS can be heard sucking termites through their muzzles from up to 330 feet away.

JELLYFISH sometimes eat other jellyfish.

The insects **BIRDS** prefer to eat are speedy and hard to catch, so oftentimes they settle for worms.

The bananas humans eat have a lot more sugar and calories than the ones monkeys consume in the wild.

While diets differ for monkeys depending on their species, fruit is something most of them can agree on. This is because of their habitats. Forests are filled with hundreds of different fruits, and as seasons change, monkeys move around to find the freshest foods. Monkeys even spread the seeds of fruit so that more will grow!

THAT'S GROSS

If you think all animals are cute and cuddly, you might want to take a closer look (or at least wash your hands)!

Doing Their Doodie

Certain **TURTLES** can breathe through their rear ends!

EASTERN PAINTED TURTLE

Animals such as **MONKEYS** and **BIRDS** search through <u>dung</u> for insects to eat.

Owl pellets aren't actually feces—<u>they're vomit.</u> Because **OWLS** often eat prey whole, they regurgitate indigestible parts, such as the fur and bones, in pellet form.

Unlike most other animal waste, **BIRD** feces is white. Because birds don't urinate, everything they emit gets mixed together, resulting in the white color.

This **WOMBAT** at the Columbus Zoo lives in the nocturnal building. Did you know wombat waste is cube-shaped?

Female **TAHRS** have been known to pee on males.

Tahrs are hooved Asian herbivores that are related to mountain goats. They usually live in rocky areas with shrubs or forests nearby. There are three different species of tahr: the Arabian, the Nilgiri and the Himalayan, which is shown here. Unfortunately, the Arabian tahr and the Nilgiri tahr are in danger of becoming extinct.

Blood? Yuck!

Rather than blood, filtered **SEAWATER** runs through sea stars' bodies.

In just one year, a colony of **100 VAMPIRE BATS** could drink all the blood of **25 COWS.**

HORNED LIZARDS
squirt blood from thin vessels around their eyes as a defense mechanism.

HIPPOS release a pinkish-reddish fluid that serves as natural sunblock but looks like bloody sweat!

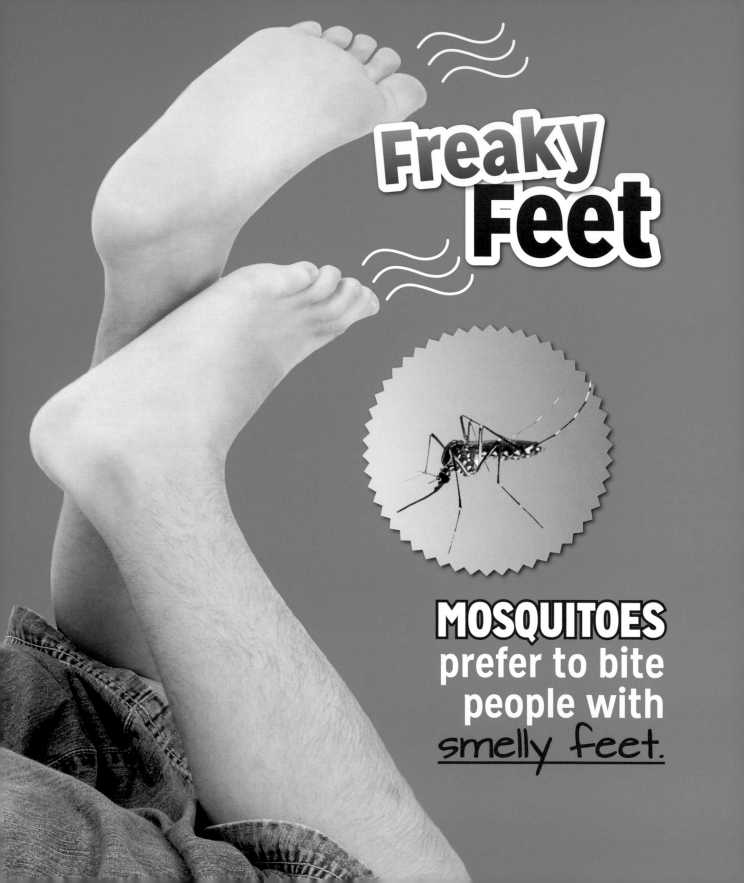

Freaky Feet

MOSQUITOES prefer to bite people with *smelly feet.*

The **BAIRD'S TAPIR**, also called a "mountain cow" or a "jungle horse," has four toes on each of its front feet and three toes on each of its back feet.

OKAPIS mark their territory with a tar-like substance that comes out of the scent glands on their feet.

Much like their relative the giraffe, okapis have huge tongues, usually between 14 and 18 inches long. They use their lengthy tongues to clean their other facial features like their eyelids and ears. Sounds like they could use some mouthwash!

Hairy Situations

CHILEAN ROSE HAIR TARANTULAS put their super hairy bodies to use when defending themselves. To fend off threats, they shoot barbed hairs at their attackers' eyes and skin.

Tiny mites live in our eyebrows.

HONEYBEES have HAIR ON THEIR EYEBALLS.

BEARDED PIGS' snouts are covered by big, bushy mustaches.

Icky Insects

FLIES vomit when they land on food! This helps them break meals into a soup-like substance they can easily suck through their tongues, which are shaped like straws.

ASSASSIN BUGS camouflage their scent by decorating themselves in the corpses of their prey.

Capuchin monkeys make their own insect repellent out of crushed **MILLIPEDES.**

DADDY LONGLEGS aren't technically spiders. Like spiders, they're arachnids, but they don't have a second body section, which is a requirement for a spider.

STINK BUGS only smell after they've been crushed.

DUNG BEETLES FEED ON THE UNDIGESTED BITS OF FOOD IN ANIMAL WASTE.

Nearly everywhere there is poop, there are dung beetles. These bugs are divided into three groups: rollers, dwellers and tunnelers. Roller dung beetles shape pieces of the waste into balls and roll them away from the pile. Tunnelers dig holes under the piles to bury pieces, and dwellers live inside the piles.

Accidental Eating

Because the **BLOBFISH** has almost no muscle, it usually eats any edible matter that floats into its mouth.

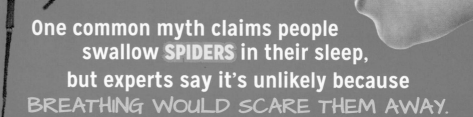

One common myth claims people swallow **SPIDERS** in their sleep, but experts say it's unlikely because BREATHING WOULD SCARE THEM AWAY.

FISH EGGS sometimes hatch in their fathers' mouths.

Father fish are not the only ones who put aquatic eggs in their mouths. Some humans do, too. But instead of protecting the eggs in their mouths, people eat fish eggs! Known as roe or caviar, edible fish eggs provide Vitamin D, much like chicken eggs and cold-water fish do. Roe and caviar also contain Vitamin B12, which is great brain food.

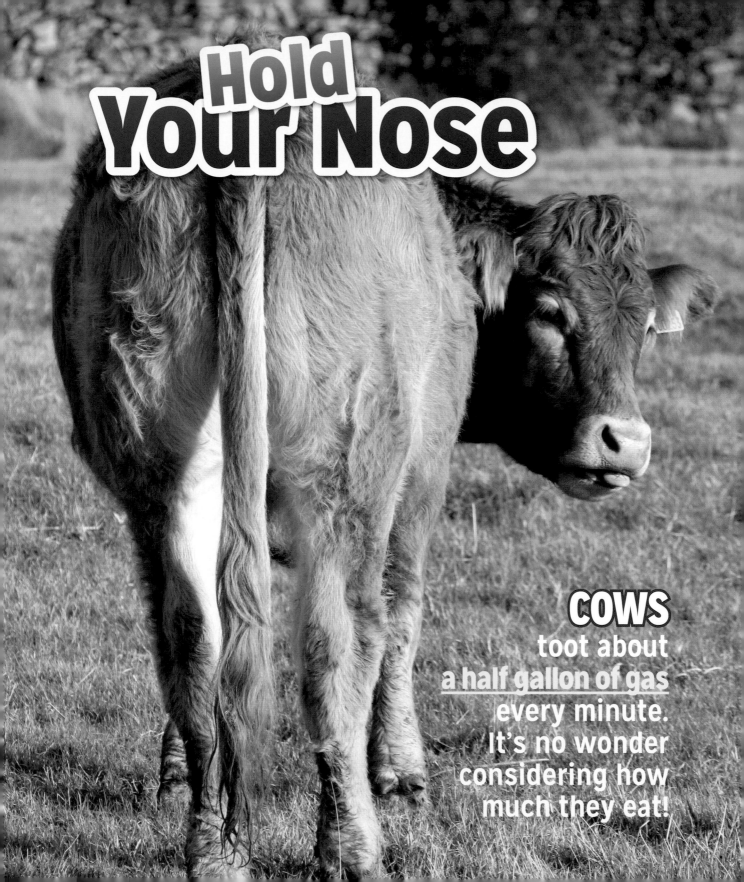

Hold Your Nose

COWS

toot about <u>a half gallon of gas</u> every minute. It's no wonder considering how much they eat!

The smelly spray **SKUNKS** use when they feel threatened contains <u>sulphuric thiols</u>, the same tear-inducing compound found in <u>raw onions.</u>

STRIPED POLECATS are like skunks but smellier. Their stench can be picked up from almost half a mile away.

The **HOATZIN**, a tropical Amazon bird, smells like manure. This trait has earned it the nickname "stink bird." Its digestive system is to blame.

Sticky and Slimy

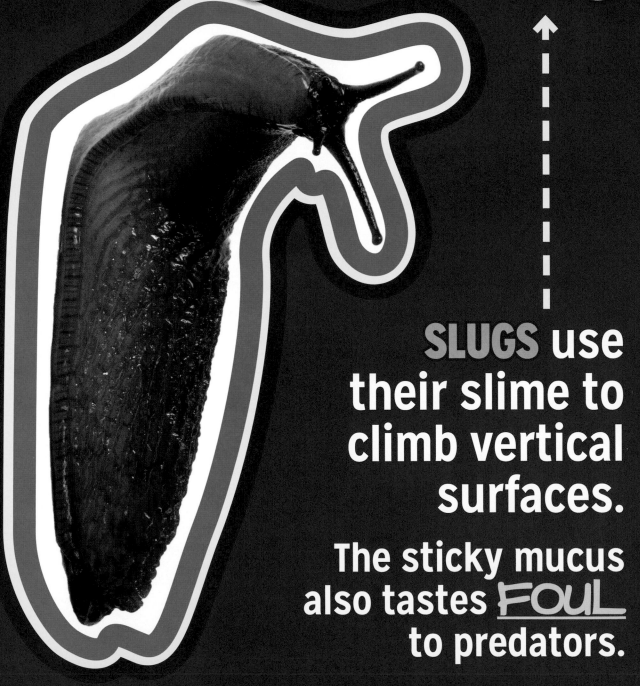

SLUGS use their slime to climb vertical surfaces.

The sticky mucus also tastes **FOUL** to predators.

The **HAGFISH** lets out as much as 17 pints of gooey mucus at once as a defense mechanism.

Before **PARROTFISH** go to sleep, they make a bed of their own mucus.

Nasty Noses

GIRAFFES clean out their nostrils with their giant tongues.

Some studies suggest **91** percent of **ADULT HUMANS** pick their noses

EMPIRICAL EVIDENCE SUGGESTS THE PERCENTAGE IS HIGHER AMONG HUMAN CHILDREN.

ELEPHANT SHREWS use their long noses to suck up worms, spiders and other bugs.

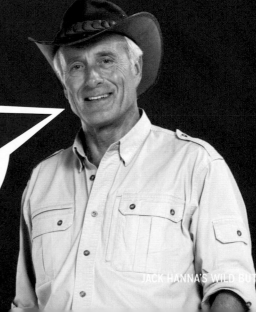

Experts have found elephant shrews to be closely related to the group of African mammals that include sea cows, elephants and aardvarks. The "elephant" part of their name comes from their long, trunk-like noses. Speaking of noses, elephant shrews produce a strong odor with their tails, which is offensive to the nostrils of would-be predators.

Male
SEAHORSES
give birth!

WEIRD AND WACKY

Absolutely odd and wonderfully wild, these animals are noteworthy for their abnormality!

Seahorses are fish, even though they don't look like it! With a tail like a monkey's, a pouch like a kangaroo's and a head like a horse's, seahorses probably look the way they do to help them quickly catch prey by surprise. Seahorses use their snouts as straws to suck up tiny fish and crustaceans—as many as 3,000 per day—for food.

Loud and Proud

Like dogs, **PIRANHAS** bark.

When they're ready to hatch from their eggs, baby **ALLIGATORS** bark!

HOWLER MONKEYS
are so loud their cries can be heard from 3 miles away!

They make booming sounds to let other howlers know an area has been claimed by a troop.

Both **LIONS** and **TIGERS** can roar as loud as <u>114 decibels.</u>

THAT'S AS LOUD AS
A LIVE ROCK CONCERT!

I love hearing the Columbus Zoo's lions roar—you can hear them from miles away!

BLACK-CAPPED CHICKADEES get their name from the sound they make:

CHICK-A-DEE-DEE-DEE!

The more danger they're in, the more **"dees"** they add to each chirp.

ROOSTERS crow at dawn in order of their social rank.

PARROTS don't have vocal cords, but many can still talk. Birds such as crows, mynah and ravens can talk, too, but parrots are best at it. They use their throat muscles to imitate speech to fit in with people or other animals.

Parrots don't always look like the one shown here. In fact, there are more than 350 different kinds, and only some of them can talk! This guy's a scarlet macaw, but parakeets, cockatoos and lovebirds are parrots, too. Despite their differences, all parrots share a few characteristics. They have curved beaks, four-toed feet and fruit-based diets.

Catching Some ZZZZZZZ'S

BATS usually sleep for about 20 hours per day.

No one's sure why people count **SHEEP** instead of cats or cows, but the dull routine is meant to lull us to sleep.

Animals don't just hibernate when it gets cold. Some desert animals, such as certain **LEMURS** and spotted tortoises, fall dormant when it gets too hot. The trick is called <u>estivation</u>.

BECAUSE SOME BIRDS MIGRATE FOR SIX MONTHS AT A TIME, THEY CAN <u>SLEEP IN FLIGHT!</u>

Z Z Z Z Z Z Z Z

ARCTIC TERN

Yawns are contagious for **CHIMPANZEES** just like they are for humans.

What's My Name?

A group of **RHINOS**, like these at *the Wilds* in Ohio, is called a **crash**.

A FEMALE ELEPHANT IS CALLED A COW.

Another name for a **ROOSTER** is a **chanticleer**.

The scientific name for a **GORILLA** is *Gorilla gorilla*!

Colo, the first gorilla born in human care in 1956 at the Columbus Zoo, became the oldest gorilla living in a zoo in 2008!

A group of **SEAGULLS** is called a squabble.

A GROUP OF CROWS IS CALLED A <u>MURDER.</u>

A group of **GIRAFFES** is called a tower!

A GROUP OF FERRETS IS CALLED A <u>BUSINESS.</u>

When wild ferrets hunt prey, they mean business—pun intended! These little guys stop at nothing when it comes time to catch the small animals they enjoy at mealtime. The intelligent mammals are so good at zeroing in on prey that the term "ferret out" has come to mean to find something by careful, persistent pursuit.

Home sweet Home

BEAVER homes are called lodges.

Some **OCTOPUSES** collect shells to display outside their homes for decoration.

About 80 PERCENT of the world's insect species live in TROPICAL RAIN FORESTS.

80%

TrueSurvivors

ANTS have been on Earth for about **140 million years.** Our species, *Homo sapiens,* has only been around for about **100,000 years.**

The average **SHARK** lives to be about 25 years old, but some have been known to reach 100!

WHALE SHARK

SPRING PEEPER

WOOD FROGS and **SPRING PEEPERS** are two types of frogs that know how to survive winter. When the cold comes, they go underground and <u>turn into frozen frogsicles!</u> Their blood sugar serves as antifreeze to protect their organs, just like the stuff that protects a car's engine in the wintertime.

Toads have pretty great survival skills, too, and they come through in their appearance. The bumps and lumps that cover toads' bodies are pockets of poison that taste bad to amphibian-eating predators. Contrary to popular belief, these poisonous lumps aren't warts, so toads can't be blamed for those human blemishes.

Cutting Teeth

JUST LIKE HUMAN CHILDREN, KID GOATS LOSE THEIR TEETH.

HAMSTER teeth never stop growing.

TIGER SHARK

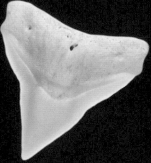

Throughout a lifetime, a **SHARK** can grow and lose up to <u>30,000 teeth.</u>

Crazy Eyes

There are about 3,000 kinds of **SNAKES** in the world, and none of them have eyelids.

BUSH VIPER

CAMELS have **3** eyelids per eye.

The pupils of a goat's eyes are rectangular.

A goat's pupils help the animal take in a field of vision of nearly 340 degrees and avoid becoming a sneaky predator's meal. They also have excellent night vision, so you won't spot many goats using flashlights! But goats' depth perception isn't as great, which means they have a hard time telling how close or far away things are.

Tongue Tied

CROCODILES' tongues are attached by a membrane that holds them in place, so <u>they can't stick out their tongues.</u>

HAWKS BILL SEA TURTLE

TURTLES can't stick out their tongues, either.

DOGS can pant 300 times per minute to cool down.

Missing Pieces

There's not a single bone in a **SHARK**'s body. They're made entirely of cartilage—the same stuff that makes up your nose and ears.

HAMMERHEAD SHARK

When they're bitten by predators, some **SEA STARS** break off their own arms. Then, they regenerate—or grow back—new ones!

JELLYFISH don't have hearts, bones, blood or brains! But they do have nerves, which help them sense things.

JELLYFISH are <u>95 percent</u> water.
HUMANS are about <u>70 percent</u> water.

Everything Else

Birds don't sweat.

GREATER ROADRUNNER

In the late 18th century, when British scientists first discovered the **PLATYPUS**, they thought the creatures were <u>so strange</u> they couldn't be <u>real!</u>

HUMAN NECKS and **GIRAFFE NECKS** are made of the same number of bones:

7

On a good spring day, a queen BEE can lay up to 2,000 eggs.

BATS are the only mammals that can fly.

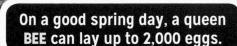

HOUSEFLIES CAN SOMERSAULT IN MIDAIR.

Killer whales aren't whales at all! They're actually a type of dolphin called an ORCA.

Orcas are the biggest members of the dolphin family. They can grow up to 32 feet long and weigh up to 6 tons. The deadly hunter has huge teeth, too. Each one can grow up to 4 inches, which is a little bit longer than a standard crayon. They use those lengthy chompers to dine on everything from seals to actual whales.

Media Lab Books
For inquiries, call 646-838-6637

Copyright 2016 Topix Media Lab

Published by Topix Media Lab
14 Wall Street, Suite 4B
New York, NY 10005

Printed in China

Paperback:
ISBN-10: 1-942556-24-1
ISBN-13: 978-1-942556-24-4
Hardcover:
ISBN-10: 1-942556-20-9
ISBN-13: 978-1-942556-20-6

CEO Tony Romando
Vice President of Sales and New Markets Tom Mifsud
Vice President of Brand Marketing Joy Bomba
Director of Finance Vandana Patel
Manufacturing Director Nancy Puskuldjian

Editor-in-Chief Jeff Ashworth
Creative Director Steven Charny **Photo Director** Dave Weiss
Content Editor Bailey Bryant
Issue Designer Elizabeth Neal
Issue Photo Editor Lindsay Pogash

Senior Editor James Ellis
Managing Editor Courtney Kerrigan
Associate Editor Tim Baker
Copy Editor Holland Baker
Assistant Editors Bailey Bryant, Trevor Courneen, Alicia Kort
Editorial Assistants Amanda Jaguden, Sarah Kim, Mara Leighton

Co-Founders Bob Lee, Tony Romando

Photo Editor Meg Reinhardt
Photo Assistant Kelsey Pillischer
Senior Designer Bryn Waryan
Designer Michelle Lock
Design Assistant Nick Harran
Junior Analyst Matthew Quinn

PHOTO CREDITS: All photos of Jack Hanna: Jack Hanna. All other photos Shutterstock and iStock except:
Suzi Hanna: p82, 116. Grahm Jones/Columbus Zoo and Aquarium: p41, 69, 88, 131, 153, 158, 159. Rick A. Prebeg/World Class
Images: p16, 17, 56, 79, 85, 117, 120. James Joel: p142. Design Pics Inc/Alamy: p6. Frans Lanting Studio/Alamy: p7. Solvin
Zankl/Alamy: p10. David Fleetham/Alamy: p12. Juniors Bildarchiv GmbH/Alma: p28. Nature Picture Library/Alamy: p33.
Blickwinkel/Alamy: p37, 73. Andrew Harrington/Alamy : p38. Ger Bosma/Alamy: p44. Amanda Cotton/Alamy: p49.
Todd Mintz/Alamy: p61. Mauritius Images GmbH/Alamy: p65. Michael Patrick O'Neill/Alamy: p69. Papilio/Alamy: p71.
SPUTNIK/Alamy: p77. National Geographic Creative/Alamy:p 83. Bill Gozansky/Alamy: p101. Robert Hamilton/Alamy: p101.
Andrew Mackay/Alamy: p107. Dave Watts/Alamy: p119. Andrew Pearson/Alamy:p137. Martin Harvey/Alamy: p145.
Mark Conlin/Alamy: p147. Cbimages/Alamy: p150.